TEAM

U.S.A.

by Devra Speregen

SCHOLASTIC INC.
New York Toronto London Auckland Sydney

ISBN 0-590-45914-7

Copyright © 1992 by Scholastic Inc.
All rights reserved. Published by Scholastic Inc.

12 11 10 9 8 7 6 5   2 3 4 5 6 7/9

Printed in the U.S.A.   34

First Scholastic printing, May 1992

Book design: David Tommasino

CONTENTS

Announcing . . . The Dream Team! 3
Official Dream Team Roster 4
On Location at the 1992 Summer Olympics: Barcelona, Spain 6
"Hoops" Olympic Style: The Rules of the Game 8

The Players

Charles Barkley 10
Larry Bird 12
Patrick Ewing 14
Earvin "Magic" Johnson 16
Pull-Out Poster
Michael Jordan 18
Karl Malone 20
Chris Mullin 22
Scottie Pippen 24
David Robinson 26
John Stockton 28
Chuck Daly, Head Coach 30

Olympic Basketball: Fun Facts and Trivia 31
Medal Watch! Dream Team Scorecard 32

Photo Credits
Cover, Poster: (*Barkley*) NBA Photos; (*Bird*) Focus on Sports/Scott Cunningham; (*Ewing, Johnson, Mullin, Pippin, Robinson*) Focus on Sports; (*Jordan*) Pat Murphy-Racey/Allsport; (*Malone*) Sportschome East/West/ Brian Drake; (*Stockton*) Focus on Sports/ICDONOUGH. **Page 4:** (*Barkley, Daly*) Focus on Sports/Ron Vesely; (*Bird*) Tim Defrisco/Allsport; (*Ewing*) Focus on Sports. **Page 5:** (*Johnson*) Otto Greule/Allsport; (*Jordan*) Jim Gund/Allsport; (*Malone*) Stephen Dunn/Allsport; (*Mullin*) Sportschome East/West; (*Pippin, Robinson*) Focus on Sports; (*Stockton*) Tim Defrisco/Allsport. **Page 6:** (*both*) Sygma/Christian Maury. **Page 7:** (*left*) Sygma/ Christian Maury; (*middle and right*) Sygma/Dominique Aubert. **Page 10:** NBA Photos. **Page 11:** Focus on Sports/Ron Vesely. **Page 12:** Focus on Sports/Scott Cunningham. **Page 13:** Tim Defrisco/Allsport. **Pages 14–16:** Focus on Sports. **Page 17:** Otto Greule/Allsport. **Page 18:** Focus on Sports/Ron Vesely. **Page 19:** Jim Gund/Allsport. **Page 20:** Sportschrome East/West/Brian Drake. **Page 21:** Stephen Dunn/ Allsport. **Page 22:** Focus on Sports. **Page 23:** Sportschrome East/West. **Pages 24–27:** Focus on Sports. **Page 28:** Focus on Sports/ICDONOUGH. **Page 29:** Tim Defrisco/Allsport. **Page 30:** Focus on Sports/ Ron Vesely.

Many thanks to Deborah Thompson for photo research.

Announcing . . . The Dream Team!

September 21, 1991.

That was the date that USA Basketball president Dave Gavitt announced the names of the first 10 basketball players chosen to play on the USA men's basketball team, coined the "Dream Team," in the 1992 Summer Olympics. This marks the first time that the USA Olympic basketball team will include professional basketball players.

"This is an historic event," Gavitt told excited basketball fans at the official press conference held to announce the team. "For the first time, all of the citizens of the United States were eligible to be selected for the Olympic team, and for the first time, we're on an equal basis with all countries."

In the past, the USA Olympic basketball team consisted of only amateur players, most of whom were college players. Previous international rules forbade NBA (National Basketball Association) players from competing in the Olympics. However, on April 7, 1989, at the FIBA (Federal International Basketball Association) World Congress, the FIBA member countries voted overwhelmingly (56–13) "for open competition," making all basketball players eligible for international competition.

Now, at the XXV Olympics in Barcelona, Spain, the United States will be represented by 10 basketball heroes, all current standouts in the NBA! With such talented, popular professionals competing, the basketball competition at the 1992 Summer Games promises to be the sporting event of the year!

Four of the 10 players selected — New York Knicks' Patrick Ewing, Chicago Bulls' Michael Jordan, Golden State Warriors' Chris Mullin, and San Antonio Spurs' Dave Robinson — have been members of past Olympic teams. Jordan, Mullin, and Ewing were the top three scorers on the 1984 USA Olympic team that swept eight games to capture the gold medal in Los Angeles. Robinson was the USA leading rebounder and second-leading scorer on the 1988 USA team that won the bronze medal in Seoul, South Korea. The other six — Boston Celtics' Larry Bird, former Los Angeles Lakers' Earvin "Magic" Johnson, Philadelphia 76ers' Charles Barkley, Chicago Bulls' Scottie Pippen, and Utah Jazz teammates Karl Malone and John Stockton — are all previous NBA All-Stars.

The 1992 USA Olympic team's 12-man roster will be finalized in the spring of 1992, with the selection of two or three more players — most likely college players. Under consideration are top college players such as Shaquille O'Neal from Louisiana State, Christian Laetner from Duke, and Alonzo Mourning from Georgetown. At press time, Magic Johnson was not sure whether he would be playing on the Olympic team. In November 1991, Magic announced he had tested positive for the virus that causes AIDS and was resigning from the Lakers. If he decides not to play, he may still accompany the team to Spain.

Meanwhile, as the Summer Olympics draw near, the excitement and anticipation of seeing this awesome team go for the gold grows stronger and stronger. "It just doesn't get any better than this!" Dream Teamer Larry Bird said at the press conference. "It means a lot to represent our country, to go over there and get the job done, and get the gold back from the Russians [the 1988 Olympic gold medalists in basketball]!"

His new teammate Charles Barkley agrees. "The question isn't will we win," he said with his usual assurance, "but by how much!"

Meet the Dream Team!
OFFICIAL DREAM TEAM ROSTER

Name	Position	Height	Weight	Birth Date	NBA Team
Charles Barkley	Forward	6'6"	250	02/20/63	Philadelphia 76ers
Larry Bird	Forward	6'9"	220	12/07/56	Boston Celtics
Patrick Ewing	Center	7'0"	240	08/05/62	New York Knicks
Earvin Johnson	Guard	6'9"	220	08/14/59	Los Angeles Lakers
Michael Jordan	Guard	6'6"	198	02/17/63	Chicago Bulls
Karl Malone	Forward	6'9"	256	07/24/63	Utah Jazz
Chris Mullin	Forward	6'7"	215	07/30/63	Golden State Warriors
Scottie Pippen	Guard/Forward	6'7"	210	09/25/65	Chicago Bulls
David Robinson	Center	7'1"	235	08/06/65	San Antonio Spurs
John Stockton	Guard	6'1"	175	03/26/62	Utah Jazz

Charles Barkley: "I'm playing for two reasons. Number one, it will be a chance to play for the greatest team ever assembled. And number two, this is the first time the pros have played for this country. There's great historical significance. Besides, I want to be the answer to a trivia question a million years from now!"

Larry Bird: "Magic Johnson, Michael Jordan, Charles Barkley, Patrick Ewing, Karl Malone . . . they're the reason I've accepted [the invitation to play on the Dream Team]. It's a great opportunity for me. I'm more excited than anybody on the team. They'll have another chance to play and I won't."

Coach Chuck Daly: "Obviously, I'm very honored to have been selected the head coach of the 1992 USA Olympic basketball team. I think any coach they [USA Basketball] could have selected from the final group of candidates would do an outstanding job. I'm looking forward to heading up a group that will bring the gold to the USA."

Patrick Ewing: "It's an honor to be selected. The 1992 team is definitely a better team than the 1984 team. It will be a great honor to play for the United States again."

Magic Johnson: "I must have pictured this a million times in my head. . . . Hearing the national anthem and seeing our flag raised as the gold goes around my neck. I can't describe how thrilled I am, how blessed I feel, to be chosen to be a part of this."

Michael Jordan: "We're going over there and bringing home the gold!"

Karl Malone: "I'm honored and delighted to go. Any time you have the opportunity to represent your country, it's an honor. If I can serve my country in any way, I'm glad to do it. We're going to bring back the gold."

Chris Mullin: "It's a thrill. I don't like to think about going *too* much, because it's kind of mind-boggling. I've got to step back and try to enjoy it."

Scottie Pippen: "I got the call and my answer was a straight-out yes. I didn't have any second thoughts about playing with people who I had always looked up to as a kid."

David Robinson: "Definitely, this is exciting and it's a thrill for me to be on this team. I've had a chance to play in two All-Star Games with these guys, and I can't imagine what it's going to be like when they are even more serious! I played on the '88 [Olympic] team and we came up a little short. It'll be great to go back with this team and get another shot."

John Stockton: "I'm really looking forward to the opportunity to play for the United States in the Olympics. I tried out for the Olympics when I was in college and I was cut at the last cut. It was one of the biggest disappointments in my life. Almost making the team, coming that close, was just a really big frustration. I never thought the opportunity to play in the Olympics would fall back in my lap like this."

Barcelona'92

1992 Summer Olympic
flag and mascots

The city of Barcelona and the harbor

Every four years, athletes from many nations come together to compete in what is now known as the Olympic Games. With two major competitions — one for winter sporting events (like skiing, bobsledding, and skating) and one for summer events (like swimming, basketball, and track and field) — the Olympic Games have become a symbol of goodwill among nations.

Nearly 3,000 years ago (in 776 B.C.), a cook named Coroebus won a 210-yard race against some of the best athletes in Greece. That race was the first Olympic event. Those ancient Games were very different from the Games we see on television today. Back then, there were only two competitions: a long-distance race and a sprint. And the winners at the ancient Games didn't receive medals; they were awarded an olive wreath that was placed on their heads!

Of course, there have been many changes in the Olympic Games throughout the course of history. Early Olympic events included chariot racing, the *diskos* hurl, and the *hoplitodromos* (where athletes had to run wearing armor!), while today's modern Games include such newly recognized events as Tai Kwon Do and baseball. This summer in Barcelona, 6,000 athletes will compete in 236 events in 25 different sports!

Barcelona, Spain, is the picturesque host city of the 1992 Summer Games. It takes the host country's Olympic Committee several years to prepare! There are stadia and other sports facilities to build, as well as hotels for all the spectators who come to watch the Games. In 1990, it was determined that Atlanta, Georgia, would host the 1996 Summer Games. They've already begun preparation!

In Barcelona, they've been gearing up for the 1992 Games since 1988. The people of this historical Spanish city are honored to be hosting the XXV Olympic Games, which will be held July 25–August 9, 1992. With dozens of new venues (sites) erected for the events, Barcelona is in tip-top shape for what's to come. In fact, two new access roads to the heart of the city have been built in order to alleviate traffic congestion! A pretty smart move, since they anticipate that nearly half a million sports fans will come to Barcelona to see the Games. The people of Barcelona are also set to host the grand, traditional Olympic festivals and exhibitions that take place before and after the Games. One of those traditional festivals, the Olympic Arts Festival, will be held this spring, with folklore events, classical and pop music concerts, opera, dance, and theater performances. And, as a host country, the Barcelona Olympic Committee has created an enormous, elaborate Olympic Village, designed to house the 6,000 athletes who will come to participate in the 1992 Summer Games.

Olympics: Barcelona, Spain

The Olympic stadium at night

The gymnasium

The pool

The Olympic Flag

The Olympic flag was first raised at the VII Olympics in 1920. It has been part of the Olympic tradition ever since. The white flag shows five different-colored rings: blue, yellow, black, green, and red on a field of white. The rings represent five continents — Europe, Asia, Australia, Africa, and the Americas — and the colors represent the flags of all nations. The rings are linked, symbolizing the sporting friendship of all the countries. The flag is raised during the Opening Ceremonies of the Games, accompanied by the release of white doves — a symbol of peace.

Past Summer Olympics Host Cities and Countries

XVII	1960	Rome, Italy
XVIII	1964	Tokyo, Japan
XIX	1968	Mexico City, Mexico
XX	1972	Munich, Germany
XXI	1976	Montreal, Canada
XXII	1980	Moscow, U.S.S.R.
XXIII	1984	Los Angeles, U.S.A.
XXIV	1988	Seoul, South Korea

The Olympic Medal

Pictured on the front of all Olympic medals — gold, silver, and bronze — is a Greek goddess and the Colosseum in Rome. These images have been on the face of Olympic medals since 1908. The image on the reverse side of the medals changes each Olympics. (The gold medal itself is actually gold-plated.)

The Olympic Torch

The most exciting event at the Opening Ceremonies is the lighting of the Olympic flame. The Olympic torch will be lit in the valley of Olympia in Greece, where the ancient Games were held. Then, thousands of relay runners will take turns transporting the lit torch through many countries, making their way toward Barcelona. The final runner (whose identity is kept secret until the last moment) will carry the torch into the Olympic stadium, circle the track amidst a cheering crowd of thousands, climb the steps to a spot where a huge torch has been constructed, and officially open the Games by lighting the Olympic flame. This custom began back in 1936.

"Hoops" Olympic Style:

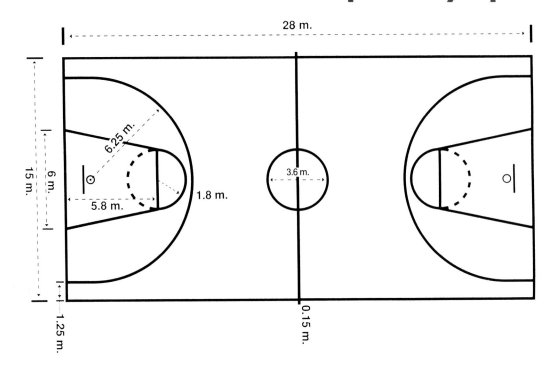

BASKETBALL RULE DIFFERENCES

	NBA	NCAA	FIBA
Periods	Four 12-minute quarters 2:10 break	Two 20-minute halves	Two 20-minute halves
Halftime	Set clock at 14 minutes Play begins at 15 minutes	15 minutes	10 minutes unless teams mutually agree to 15
Timeouts (TOs)	Seven 1:40 TOs 4-TO limit last quarter 3-TO limit last 2 minutes One 20-second TO per half noncumulative	Five 1:15 TOs One TO per overtime period	Two 1-minute TOs per half noncumulative One TO per overtime
Bonus	Fifth foul per quarter is 2-shot foul Offensive fouls are not team fouls	Bonus on seventh foul	Bonus on eighth foul No shot on offensive team-control foul
Overtime	5-minute OT 1:40 break	5-minute OT 1-minute break	5-minute OT 2-minute break
Foul Limit	6	5	5
3-Point Line	23'9" at top of key 22' at corner	19'9"	20'6.1" (6.25 m)

The Rules of the Game

The Federal International Basketball Association (FIBA) World Congress has approved a number of rule changes for the 1990–1994 basketball seasons. The new rule changes have been designed to keep pace with the ever-changing modern game of basketball, the speed and physical skills of today's athletes, and the desire to make the game challenging for the players and exciting for the spectators.

Here are some of the more important changes:

- **Team Bench Area:** A team bench area will be marked on the floor. The area will extend from a point five meters from the center line to the end line. Players and coaches may only leave this area for certain specified reasons.

- **Substitutes:** A player becomes a substitute at the time the official beckons that player's replacement onto the floor.

- **Uniforms:** Undergarments that extend below the shorts may be worn, provided they are the same single color as the shorts.

- **Coaches:** Only the coach and his assistants may communicate with table officials during the game.

- **Duties of Timekeeper:** The consultive process to be followed by the referee at the end of a period has been changed. Should the officials not hear the signal, the referee shall consult with the umpire and, if necessary, the other table officials. However, the referee shall make the final decision.

- **In Case of Injury to Players and Officials:** If an injured player cannot continue to play immediately and receives treatment, he must be substituted within one minute, or as soon as possible should the injury prevent an earlier substitution.

- **Substitutions:** Once the ball has gone into play for the first or only free throw, no substitutions are allowed unless a foul or violation is called before the clock starts.

- **Dribbling:** A fumble has been defined as "Accidentally losing and then regaining player control [fumble] at the beginning or end of a dribble."

- **Technical Foul by Player:** Leaving the court to gain an unfair advantage has now been included under the technical foul article.
  The definition of "grasping the ring" (rim of the basket) has been expanded to state, "Grasping the ring in such a way that the weight of the player is supported by the ring." Grasping the ring is a technical foul unless, in the judgment of the official, the player is trying to prevent injury to himself or another player.

- **Personal Foul:** Hand-checking has now been included in the rules and is the action by a defensive player in a guarding situation where the hand(s) are used to contact an opponent to either impede the player's progress or to assist the defensive player in guarding his/her opponent. Such contact is illegal as it gives unfair advantage to the defensive player.

- **Double Foul:** A double foul is now defined as "two opposing players" commiting fouls against each other at the same time.

- **Fighting:** Bench personnel who leave the team bench area during a fight, or any situation that may lead to a fight shall be disqualified from the game and banished from the vicinity of the court.
  A coach may leave the team bench area, but only in order to assist the officials to maintain or restore order.

Charles Barkley

When he was a kid, Charles Barkley's friends used to laugh at him when he told them he would someday play in the NBA. Now, as the fiercest rebounder and leading scorer of the Philadelphia 76ers, and as part of the superstar 1992 USA Olympic basketball team, it's Charles who is having the last laugh!

Charles has had to work extra hard to become such an awesome player. When he didn't make his high school basketball team, he could have thrown in the towel, but he didn't. Instead, he threw himself into a vigorous training schedule. Every day after school, Charles worked at improving his basketball skills. He strengthened his jumping ability by leaping over a four-foot-high fence in his backyard — sometimes for hours at a time! And at night, it was off to a nearby playground for hours more, working to perfect his shooting and rebounding. "I made up my mind a long time ago to be successful at whatever I did," said Charles. "If you want to be successful, nobody can stop you."

Fortunately, his persistence paid off. By his junior year in high school, Charles finally made the team. In his senior year, he had become such an outstanding player that he earned himself a basketball scholarship to Auburn University in Alabama.

At Auburn, Charles was a celebrity on the team. Already a powerhouse on the court, he gained even more attention by leading the Southeastern Conference in rebounding for three seasons in a row and helping Auburn to a 20–11 record in 1984.

That year, the Philadelphia 76ers selected Charles for their team in the first round of the NBA draft, making him the fifth selection overall. They were glad they did, too, since his awesome rebounds and scoring helped lead the 76ers to the Eastern Conference finals that season. Charles has been a star to 76ers' fans ever since. He has led the team in rebounding for five seasons, and in scoring for four. And in the 1989–1990 season, it was his consistently high scoring that helped the 76ers finish first in the Atlantic Division. The other players in the league chose Charles as NBA Player of the Year that season.

Today, Charles Barkley is one of the most — if not the most — powerful forwards in the NBA. So powerful in fact, that he once slam-dunked the ball so hard, the entire basket moved six inches! The basket — backboard, stand, and all — weighed 2,240 pounds! He's played in five NBA All-Star Games, was selected Most Valuable Player of the 1991 NBA

All-Star Game, and is among the league's Top 10 scorers each year. Not bad for someone who had trouble making his high school team!

What's this Alabama native like off the court? Well, for starters, Charles is quite the family man. He lives with his wife, Maureen, and his three-year-old daughter, Christiana Michelle, in Bala Cynwyd, Maryland. Admittedly, some of his favorite things to do, when he's not with his family or playing basketball, include watching soap operas (his favorite is *The Young and the Restless*), playing golf, and entertaining friends at home. He also had fun appearing on TV! In the past, Charles has appeared in commercials for Nike and Right Guard, and has guest-appeared on the *Arsenio Hall Show*, *Late Night with David Letterman*, and *thirtysomething*.

For this 6'6" shooter who wears a size-15½ shoe, having fun is what life is all about. He certainly has fun playing basketball! "If you're having fun," he says, "it makes you play better. When you're happy, you get a little bit of extra energy."

Larry Bird

Thirty-five-year-old Larry Bird may be the oldest basketball player on the Olympic Dream Team but he admits that he is probably more excited than any of his teammates to play in Barcelona this summer. Why? Because it will most likely be Larry's last chance to compete in the Olympics. "They'll all get the chance again," he said, "and this is my only chance." Even though some people speculate on Larry's ability to play well since undergoing back surgery last June, Larry reports that he has been working out since September and is raring to go! "I feel better now than I have in three or four years," he said.

A forward with the Boston Celtics, Larry Bird is by far one of the greatest basketball players of all time. Mentioned in the same breath as Magic Johnson and Kareem Abdul-Jabbar, there is no question that whenever this sharpshooter does decide to hang up his Celtics uniform and retire (something he says he's going to do nearly every season!), his name will go down as one of the greats in the history of pro basketball.

Larry made it to the pros after a remarkable college career at Indiana State University. He helped put that school on the map, leading the ISU Sycamores to an 81–13 record in three years, and to a spot in the 1979 NCAA finals. His list of accomplishments at ISU is quite impressive, but it's still nothing compared to what he's achieved with the Celtics.

In Boston, Larry Bird is a legend. Drafted by the Celtics in the first round of the 1978 draft, he was voted NBA Rookie of the Year in 1980. He was named to the All-Star Team his first nine years (10 times total!) and was the NBA Most Valuable Player in 1984, 1985, and 1986. On top of that, he has averaged more than 10 rebounds a game during his career, while averaging six assists and two steals. There isn't a seat available at the Boston Garden (where the Celtics play) and there hasn't been for the past 10 seasons. And it's all because of Larry.

Honest, loyal, steadfast, dependable . . . these are just a few of the words used to describe Number 33. "Larry has a way of making everybody he comes in contact with a better person," his friend and lawyer, Bob Woolfe, says. "If you think the Larry Bird on the court has character and is unselfish — well, off the court he is even more so." Celtics' general manager Red Auerbach has even gone as far as to say that Larry is "the greatest ballplayer who ever played the game."

Of course, in Boston, Larry Bird is the most talked about and admired athlete, but this holds true in other parts of the country as well. Especially in Indiana, where he's from. Bird-mania is so rampant in the Hoosier State, that the Indiana newspapers and radio frequently feature the Boston Celtics over the Indiana Pacers! Larry owns a hotel and restaurant in Indiana, where patrons can buy Larry Bird memorabilia (Larry Bird golf balls, Larry Bird shower curtains, Larry Bird chocolates, etc.) as well as a Ford-Lincoln-Mercury dealership. Off-season, he prefers to live in his Indiana hometown of West Baden with his wife, Dinah, in a house not too far from the one he grew up in.

Larry is proud of where he came from, and his West Baden neighbors are equally proud of their hometown hero. So proud, in fact, that they recently named a street after him! Larry Bird Boulevard now runs straight through West Baden, from one end of town to the other!

Patrick Ewing

"The guy is just incredible. They say you're at Michael Jordan's mercy when he gets the ball. Well, it's the same with Patrick. He's simply unstoppable."

That's Trent Tucker, Ewing's former New York Knicks' teammate talking, but plenty of others share the same opinion of Patrick Ewing, the seven-foot power center.

No wonder this former Georgetown University Hoya whom they called "The Hoya Destroyer" was selected to play on the Olympic Dream Team — he's a sure thing!

This won't be the first time Patrick has donned the USA basketball uniform. Along with pals Michael Jordan and Chris Mullin, he was a member of the U.S. team that won the gold medal at the Los Angeles Olympic Games in 1984. "With a team like this," Patrick said of the assembly of talent for this summer's team, "there's no question we will do it again."

A native of Kingston, Jamaica, Patrick came to the United States with his parents at age 11. Voted High School Player of the Year at his school in Cambridge, Massachusetts, Patrick was offered a scholarship to Georgetown University. He played with the GU Hoyas for four years, picking up the Adolph Rupp, the Eastman Kodak, and the Naismith awards as College Player of the Year (1985) in the process. At Georgetown, Patrick set career records with 1,316 rebounds and 493 blocked shots, while his 2,184 points ranked second. He graduated from Georgetown with a degree in fine arts.

Today, many agree that Patrick Ewing is the best player on the New York Knicks. He is 240 pounds of muscle, hardened by a strict workout regimen of five-times-a-week weight-training sessions — all year long. A huge man, Patrick's on court presence is something to be reckoned with. His "weapons" include a jump hook with either hand and a deadly turnaround baseline jumper. To his teammates, he is known as "Boomer" because of his slamming one-handed dunks. To his friends and family, he is simply Patrick.

Patrick lives in Fort Lee, New Jersey, during the season, and Potomac, Maryland, during the off-season with his wife, Rita, and his one-year-old daughter, Randi. He also has a six-year-old son, Patrick Ewing, Jr., who lives with his mother in Boston. A genuinely likeable guy, Patrick is involved in all sorts of projects. As a "movie star," he has had two motion picture cameo roles. He has also appeared

on TV's *Webster* with Emmanuel Lewis, *Late Night with David Letterman,* and as a guest VeeJay on MTV. As for sneakers, you won't see Patrick doing Nike or Reebok commercials — he has his own line of sneakers called Patrick Ewing 33.

Since 1989, Patrick has put his awesome talents for blocking shots to a doubly good use. In conjunction with Voit Sports, Patrick donates $100 to a charity for every shot he blocks at a home game. The past two seasons, he donated nearly $61,000 to the Children's Health fund, which provides free health care to homeless children in New York. This year, he is donating $100 for every blocked shot to the Boys' Club of New York.

What's his motivation to play so intensely? Basically, this explosive scoring and blocking machine wants to be remembered. "I want to be the best," he says. "I want to have people mention me in the same breath with Wilt Chamberlain and Bill Russell, or maybe say I'm better!"

15

Earvin "Magic" Johnson

On November 7, 1991, the world received the sad news that basketball star extraordinaire Magic Johnson would be hanging up his Converse sneakers and leaving the game. The 6'9" dynamo, who is one of the greatest basketball players of all time, tested positive for the virus that causes AIDS, and decided to retire.

The announcement came not too long after the Dream Team selections were made public. Naturally, Magic had been one of the first NBA stars selected to play in Barcelona but, as this publication went to press, he was still undecided if he would take to the court this summer in Spain. Regardless of his decision, Magic has made it clear to his fans that he doesn't intend to disappoint them or his Dream Team teammates. Whether or not he decides to take to the court this summer, he intends to be in Barcelona supporting the Dream Team in every way he can.

It's no wonder Magic Johnson has such a talent for hoops. Both his parents played the sport in high school, and both were quite good! By the time he was in the fourth grade, Magic was shooting hoops with his father and older brother every Sunday. He loved playing so much that, even when it snowed, he would shovel the court at the Main Street Elementary School in Lansing, Michigan, just so he could practice!

How did he get the nickname "Magic"? It wasn't until he was on the basketball team at Everett High that he earned that tag. It was during his freshman year, after a particularly spectacular game where he recorded a triple double (36 points, 18 rebounds, and 14 assists) and stole the ball five times. A sportswriter named Fred Stabley told him he needed a nickname that would describe his remarkable talents. "How do you like the name Magic?" Stabley asked. "It's fine," answered a grinning Earvin. He's been called Magic ever since.

Faced with dozens of college scholarship offers, Magic chose to attend Michigan State University and play basketball with the MSU Spartans. He had become somewhat of a celebrity during his high school basketball career, and plenty of local fans were happy about his decision to stay in Michigan. In fact, the day after he announced his intent to attend MSU, there was a mad rush for season tickets!

Magic performed beautifully in college — both on the court and in the classroom. He led the Spartans to two Big Ten championship wins and one

NCAA championship for which he was named the tournament's Most Valuable Player. In addition to hours of practice, he also studied for three to four hours a day.

In 1979, the Los Angeles Lakers owned the rights to the number-one selection in the college draft. Since Magic had decided to leave school at that time (promising his mother he would finish his education during off-seasons), the Lakers made the star player an offer.

Now, after 12 glorious years with the Lakers and shelves full of numerous awards and accolades (NBA Most Valuable Player: 1987, 1989, 1990; NBA Play-off MVP: 1980, 1982, 1987; NBA All-Star Game MVP: 1990 — to name just a few), Magic Johnson's professional basketball career may be over. But one thing is definitely for sure — in the hearts of basketball fans everywhere, the Magic will go on forever!

Michael Jordan

1991 was an excellent year for Michael "Air" Jordan. On June 12, he finally achieved a lifelong dream: to win the NBA championship! Season after season, this 6'6" slam-dunking machine came close, but never won. On that fateful June night, in the fifth game against the Los Angeles Lakers, Air Jordan finally led the Bulls to victory!

This year, Michael has a new dream. As a member of this summer's USA Olympic basketball team, he desperately wants to win gold — and to reclaim the championship from the Soviets. It wouldn't be Michael's first Olympic gold medal, though — he played on the winning 1984 USA Olympic basketball team, alongside Dream Team teammates Patrick Ewing and Chris Mullin. "I already know what to expect," Michael said, "and I feel very confident. We have a great team assembled — great players and great coaches. I know we'll be bringing home the gold!"

Yes, Michael certainly sounds determined. In fact, determination is something this 29-year-old has had all his life. Even as a young boy, Michael was the most driven in his family. He wouldn't give up at anything until he got what he wanted. Especially when it came to basketball. Michael didn't make the high school basketball team when he first tried out, and he watched in envy as his older brother Larry became the star of that team. Michael made practice a priority in his life, hitting the courts for two hours every day after school, and all day on weekends.

Eventually, Michael did make the high school team. In his senior year, Michael followed in Larry's footsteps, becoming Laney High's star player!

After high school, Michael went to the University of North Carolina on a basketball scholarship. It was there, in his freshman year, that he became famous after nailing a 17-foot jump shot with 16 seconds left in the 1982 NCAA national championships. He stayed only one more season with the UNC Tar Heels, before joining the NBA.

Today, Michael Jordan is not only the Chicago Bulls' star player, but one of the best in the NBA. He repeatedly astounds audiences all over the country by seemingly defying the laws of gravity while scoring. And indeed, Number 23 has redefined the meaning of "slam-dunk."

Both on and off the court, Michael is one of the most visible personalities in the world. Aside from the cool $3.7 million he earns each year from the

Bulls, Michael reportedly brings in an additional $11 million a year as a spokesman for commercial products. He has his own line of gym shoes, sportswear, bubble gum, and greeting cards.

Michael has used his celebrity status as a way to help the less fortunate. In 1989, he founded the Michael Jordan Foundation, which supports a variety of charities. In addition, he responds to hundreds of requests from sick children who want to meet him, and he participates in hundreds of charity events every year. "It's a big blessing," he says. "I feel obligated to give something back so that others can stumble upon their dreams. That's how I did it — I stumbled upon it."

At home, Michael is also a superstar — a superstar dad and a superstar husband. Off-season, he enjoys living the simple life — spending time with his wife, Juanita, and his son, Jeffrey. He especially enjoys cooking, listening to music (Anita Baker and Luther Vandross), watching mystery movies, collecting cars (he has over a dozen!), and playing golf. Michael loves to play golf so much, he has a six-hole putting green in his basement! He has hopes of one day turning pro in that sport as well.

Karl Malone

By now, almost everyone knows why they call Karl Malone, the rock-hard forward of the Utah Jazz, "The Mailman." But for those of you who don't, it's because, when this 6'9" NBA All-Star takes to the basketball court, he "delivers."

Born on July 24, 1963, in Summerfield, Louisiana, Karl was the eighth child (of nine) born to his parents, Shirley and J.P. His father died of bone cancer when Karl was just four.

"Karl was a happy and loving child," his mother says, "and always polite and respectful." Karl, in turn, has only good things to say about his mom. "I'd like to find a woman I could marry one day," he says, "but it's going to be hard to find a woman like my mother!" Mother and son have always been incredibly close. Karl likes to tell the story of how his mom would help him practice his shooting. Oh, it's not what you think. She didn't take her son out to the school yard and teach him how to shoot, she helped in a different way — by standing with her arms in a circle and acting as the basket!

Karl attended Summerfield High School in Louisiana where he made a name for himself as a decent, strong player. Ultimately, he went on to Louisiana Tech, where he made another name for himself — The Mailman. In 1985, the Utah Jazz selected The Mailman as the thirteenth player in the draft.

When he first moved to Salt Lake City, he was miserable. "He was homesick," his mom remembers. "That first month he was there, we had a $700 phone bill. He wanted to come home." All that changed on Karl's twenty-second birthday, which he shared with Pioneer Day, a major holiday in Utah. He was asked to ride a float in the annual Pioneer Day parade. Honored, he gladly accepted, and that was the beginning of a warm relationship between Karl and the people of Salt Lake City. With each passing season, Karl finds he spends more and more of his time there.

On the court, Karl Malone has become one of the NBA's best and most charismatic basketball players, though his notoriety goes far beyond his sunny disposition and his cool style. Karl has a rare combination of power and grace on the court and works extremely hard at improving himself — whether it's in striving to master three-pointers or just working out to perfect his physique. He is also known as a truly caring individual. One of his teammates once remarked that Karl has "the biggest heart in Utah."

What Karl also has is an unbelievable fascination

with cars, trucks, and airplanes — especially trucks. He drives a Chevy Silverado pickup with 40-inch tires and has "The Mailman" painted on the side doors. His dream is to buy an 18-wheeler after he retires from basketball. "Trucks have fascinated me since I was a boy," he said.

Karl loves animals, too. He currently has a dog, a rabbit, a tank full of piranhas, and another of goldfish. In the past, he has owned a pet lobster, an iguana, and some snakes. In addition to the 18-wheeler, Karl says he has hopes of owning a Texas ranch when he retires, and he dreams of stocking it with wild animals — like tigers!

But for all he has, this small-town kid from Louisiana loves sharing with others. Donating heaps of money to charities helps him remember what it was like growing up without money. "I never forget where I'm from," he says. "I saw my mother wear cardboard in her shoes, just so each of us kids could have a new pair. Nobody should have to do that."

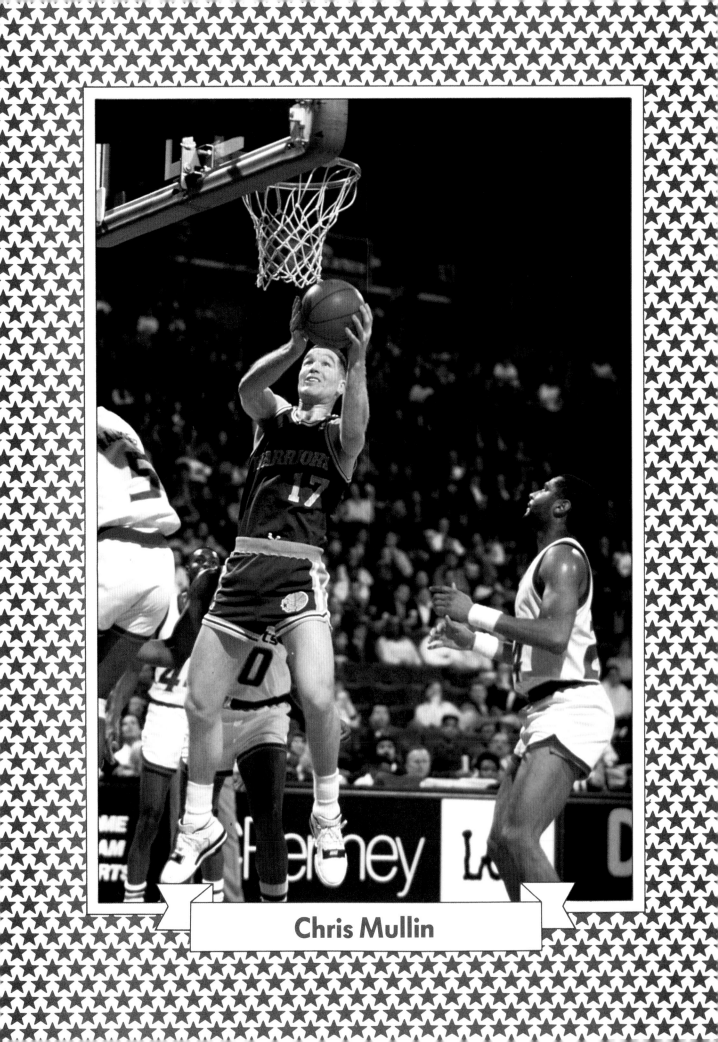

Chris Mullin

Chris Mullin was one of the top scorers on the 1984 U.S. Olympic basketball team that won the gold medal. Even so, he admits that he's still in shock from having been selected to this year's Dream Team! "It's hard to believe," Chris said. "A couple of years ago, I would never have been given a chance like this."

It's true. A few years ago, Chris Mullin realized he was an alcoholic. Not long after graduating from New York's St. John's University and signing with the Golden State Warriors in 1985, his "social" drinking began to get out of hand. By 1987, he had gained nearly 30 pounds and would often get sick to his stomach after a workout. In December of 1987, Chris's coach, Don Nelson, approached him and asked him to try and quit drinking for one month. But Chris was so far gone by then that he couldn't even last a few days without having a drink. It looked as though his promising basketball career would be coming to an end.

Later that month, with the help and support of his parents, his girlfriend, and Don Nelson, Chris checked himself into an alcohol rehabilitation hospital where he stayed until January 1988. "It's amazing how much you can learn in 28 days," he said after his release. "When I was in there, I didn't think about basketball. I hadn't been enjoying basketball. I wanted to enjoy it again."

When he was released, Chris vowed to take control of his life again. He threw himself into a strenuous workout that really helped keep him sober. Not only did he stop drinking altogether, but he also began to monitor everything he put into his body, making sure he was eating healthy, too. He worked out three to four times a day and, by January 29, he was ready to play again. By the following season, Chris had made so much progress, he was made a point forward and co-captain of the Warriors, and was chosen for the NBA All-Star Team! Today, Chris is the Warriors' leading scorer.

These days, Chris has become a physical fitness freak. He works out a few times a day and, most nights around 11 P.M., he goes to work out at the "gym." The gym is the Oakland Coliseum Arena where the Warriors play. Chris and all his teammates have keys to the arena and, on the nights it is empty, they use the equipment or just practice shooting. Chris is so dedicated, he even works out during vacations and the off-season.

After each season, Chris travels across the country to spend time with his mother in New York. When he joined the NBA in 1985, Chris moved his parents from their Brooklyn, New York, home to a big house with a pool on Long Island. It is there that he goes in the off-season to visit friends and family, and to rest up for the following season. Since his father passed away last summer, Chris really feels the need to be close to home whenever he can. Sometimes, he brings his girlfriend of eight years, Liz, back east with him.

Now, Chris is looking forward to being on the 1992 Olympic team. Lean, fit, and a steady, healthy 215 pounds, this 6'7" awesome scorer has become an integral part of the Warriors' fast-paced running game, and hopes to be an integral part of the Dream Team as well. As for enjoying the game, the "new" Chris says basketball is as much fun now as it was when he was at St. John's. Despite missing his father immensely, Chris Mullin has finally made peace with his life. "I'm probably the happiest I've ever been," he says proudly.

Scottie Pippen

When it was announced that Chicago Bulls guard/forward Scottie Pippen was invited to play on the Olympic Dream Team, the Bulls' administration worried he might actually accept the invitation. Why were they worried? Because three summers ago, Scottie had back surgery and, since he is one of their best players, they didn't want to run the risk of him injuring himself in Spain. Scottie, on the other hand, feels differently.

"It means too much to me to be on this team," Scottie said. "I've been in physical therapy for three years, and I'm feeling good. I don't want to pass up this chance." So Scottie, along with his Bulls teammate, Michael Jordan, has accepted to play for the USA.

He speaks with a comfy down-home accent and wears studious-looking wire-framed glasses off the court, but on the court he plays with a flair reserved for a select and gifted few. Sometimes, he even outshines Air Jordan.

Scottie was born and grew up in Hamburg, Arkansas, and attended the University of Central Arkansas in Conway. As a consensus National Association of Intercollegiate Athletics (NAIA) All-America in his senior year, he averaged 26.3 points and 10 rebounds per game. Originally, Scottie was to be drafted by Seattle in the 1987 NBA draft, but Seattle traded their draft rights with Chicago and Chicago drafted him. One year after joining the Bulls, he underwent back surgery and missed the entire exhibition season and first eight games of the 1988–1989 season.

Last year, Scottie's astounding on-court antics helped lead the Bulls to their first NBA championship victory. During the play-offs, Scottie was unstoppable! "The play-offs are the time you have to step up to another level," he said. He finished the 1991 play-offs ranked first on the team in rebounding (8.9) and steals (2.47), second in scoring (21.6) and assists (5.8). That season also marked a milestone in his short career: On December 27, 1990, Scottie made his 500th career steal in a game against the Golden State Warriors!

The Bulls' coach, Phil Jackson, is hesitant to say that Scottie is on Michael Jordan's level, but he does say that he is the perfect complement to Jordan. "What helps Scottie," Jackson said, "is that he's a secondary concern to most teams [playing the Bulls]. Teams focus so much on Michael, that it opens things up for Scottie."

Last summer, Scottie was rewarded by the Bulls with a generous new contract. And, although he knows he'll always be second best in Chicago basketball, he says that that knowledge keeps him on his toes. "Playing with a guy like Michael Jordan," he says, "you have to take a lot of pride in what you're doing. You don't want to fall that far behind. Even though you know you have to take a back seat to him, you always want to be a competitive player."

These days, Scottie resides in Highland Park, Illinois, but he returns to Arkansas every year to visit his family and friends. A playful personality, this 6'7", 210-pound ballplayer admits his secret ambition is to become a professional dog breeder! His favorite foods are macaroni and cheese, and cabbage greens and steak, and his off-the-court hobbies include cleaning his cars and learning to fly airplanes. Scottie says his favorite way to relax is to kick back and watch *Cosby Show* reruns.

David Robinson

You know him as the sensational center for the San Antonio Spurs, the 7'1" powerhouse they call "The Admiral," who consistently amazes fellow NBA players and fans alike with his extraordinary quickness and strength; and as the 235-pound rebound pro who receives hundreds of fan letters each day and signs countless autographs each week.

But 26-year-old David Robinson can't understand what all the fuss is about. He considers himself to be just an average guy. "It's been an adjustment being a public figure," he said. "But it's just part of my profession. The only thing I think about is being the best person I can be."

The son of a retired Navy petty officer, David was born in Key West, Florida, and grew up in Virginia. When he was a student at Osborn Park High School, his scoring was not limited to the basketball courts — he scored an impressive 1,320 on his SAT College Board Examination! Thanks to that high score, he received an appointment to the United States Naval Academy in Annapolis, Maryland, where he majored in mathematics.

A dedicated, career-minded college student, David confesses that, before basketball entered the picture, he had hopes of becoming a math teacher! "I hadn't even considered a career in the NBA when I went to Navy," he recalled. "I had my options totally open. Basketball was really a shot in the dark."

But, as David continued playing basketball at Navy, there was no denying his potential as a professional. In four years at the Academy, he established 33 Navy records before going on to play in the World and Pan American Games as well as the 1988 Olympics. Many Americans, however, remember David as the player who scored 50 points in a win over Syracuse and took a mediocre Naval Academy squad to within one game of the NCAA Final Four. In 1987, before going to the Olympics, he became the number-one selection in the NBA draft, and was snatched up by the San Antonio Spurs.

It's easy to see why David has since become such a hot property in the NBA. While just a rookie center with the Spurs, he was selected to play on the NBA All-Star Team! Not many rookies receive All-Star status. These days, David is considered to be an outstanding player on the Spurs.

Despite his tremendous success, David has managed to stay focused, keeping his head on straight and his values in the right place. His teammates all say he's a great team player. David credits the strict Navy discipline he received for his ability to work well with others. "Every night you go up against a guy you've got to be mentally tough for," he says. "I try to stay focused on what I have to do for the team — go to the boards, block shots, and play defense. I don't worry about scoring or individual statistics."

David is involved with the "I Have a Dream" Foundation. He recently gave the San Antonio chapter a $180,000 pledge. The organization offers college scholarships to elementary school children if they stay in school, go to high school, and apply to college.

At home, David enjoys reading, cooking, and listening to music. His favorite foods are lasagne, fettucine, and tacos; he likes to groove to Natalie Cole and Grover Washington, Jr.; and this big, strong Navy man admits that his all-time favorite movie is *The Little Mermaid!*

John Stockton

In a Spokane, Washington, tavern called Jack & Dan's, locals come from miles around to watch basketball on TV. But they don't come to root for the Seattle Supersonics or the Portland Trail Blazers (the two teams closest to Spokane). It is the Utah Jazz — 734 miles away — who stir this crowd.

That's all because of the Jazz's star point guard, 30-year-old John Stockton. John's father is Jack Stockton (of Jack & Dan's) and the crowd in the tavern is made up of John's hometown family and friends who remember him as the shortest, skinniest kid in the neighborhood! Now, this 6'1", 175-pound guy they used to call "Little Johnny" and "Johnny Boy" is a two-time NBA All-Star. "I'm sure the people in Spokane are surprised at what I've done," John says, "and I know they're very proud of me. They feel they had a hand in it . . . and they did."

To compensate for his lack of height as a teenager, John threw himself into a tough practice regimen. He played at school, at a local gym every morning at 6 A.M., at the YMCA, at yet another school yard, and with his brother.

After high school, John stayed in his hometown to attend Gonzaga University. By then, he had become an excellent player and a local hero. At GU, he was the first player in the school's history to score 1,000 points with 5,000 assists. Today, John is well-known for his many assists, holding records for most assists (even more than Isiah Thomas or Magic Johnson) in 1988–1990. In 1990, he set the all-time NBA record for assists in one season with 1,134. He was an All-Rookie team Honorable Mention in 1984–1985, setting Jazz rookie records for assists and steals, and he didn't miss a single game in more than five years until a badly sprained ankle sidelined him in 1990.

If ever a personality seemed perfectly matched to the unselfishness of a point guard's position, it's John Stockton. He truly seems happier giving than receiving, and prefers to remain in the background during a game, feeding the ball to his teammates so they can score. But don't get him wrong; John is also an aggressive player. "He may look like a choir boy," says Utah coach Jerry Sloan, "but I'll tell you, he busts on people if he has to."

In basketball's off-season, John still remains tight with his family. He and his wife, Nada, and their two sons live in a big house right next door to John's parents in Spokane. "He's a real down-to-earth guy," says John's brother, Steve. "He never holds

anything over your head. When the season's over, he comes home, and that's it. He's just one of the boys again."

John looks forward to the upcoming Games in Barcelona, and feels honored to have been named to the team. He is even more excited to have been chosen along with his Jazz teammate and good friend Karl Malone. The two are quite a pair — as close as brothers. On the basketball court, the duo has a certain chemistry and their teammates know it. "Karl makes the game easier for all of us," John says. "He draws so much attention to himself on the court, that it leaves a lot of us open to do other things. Without him, we'd be a drastically different team." Karl feels the exact same way about John.

Chuck Daly, Head Coach

"Any time you have a chance to do something for your country, it's an honor. This is something you don't dream will ever happen to you. It's beyond dreams, really."

These are the words of 61-year-old Chuck Daly, coach of the NBA's Detroit Pistons, who has been named head coach for the 1992 USA men's basketball team — the Dream Team. "Obviously, I'm very honored to be selected," Daly said at the press conference announcing the Dream Team players. "I'm looking forward to heading up a group that will bring the gold to the USA."

A graduate of Bloomsburg University in Pennsylvania, Daly earned his master's degree from Penn State. He was head coach at Boston College and Penn State, and he spent six years as an assistant coach at Duke University, helping lead the Blue Devils to the NCAA Final Four twice. Now, after his ninth season coaching the Pistons, he is hailed as a winning coach who has led the Pistons to back-to-back NBA championships in 1989 and 1990.

Coach Daly admits that, even with the NBA superstars on the U.S. Olympic team this summer, winning isn't going to be easy. "Anyone who thinks there's a cakewalk involved is making a serious mistake," he said. "We have taught the world how to play basketball and they have adapted very well." Furthermore, Coach Daly explains that games will be difficult to win. "These [other] teams are too good," he said, "especially with international rules. We had better go to Barcelona totally prepared, and I think everyone involved understands that."

Although he thinks the competition will be tough, Daly is still confident he has a winning crew. "I think, quite frankly, we'll be good enough to win," he said.

Head Coach: Chuck Daly (Detroit Pistons)
Assistant Coach: P. J. Carlesimo (Seton Hall University)
Assistant Coach: Mike Krzyzewski (Duke University)
Assistant Coach: Lenny Wilkens (Cleveland Cavaliers)

Olympic Basketball: Fun Facts and Trivia

• Basketball was introduced as an exhibition sport at the 1904 Olympics held in St. Louis, Missouri. The sport itself was invented 13 years before, by a Springfield, Massachusetts, gym teacher named James A. Naismith. When Naismith's students complained about another winter of boring exercises in gym class, Naismith decided to invent an indoor game for them. He asked the school janitor to nail peach baskets to the balcony railings at both ends of the gymnasium. He divided his students into two teams of nine, gave them a soccer ball, and told them to play! Each time someone scored, the janitor would bring his ladder onto the court, climb up, and take the ball from the basket. They hadn't yet thought of cutting the bottoms out of the baskets!

• The very first Olympic basketball tournament was held in 1936 in Berlin, Germany. The Games were held outdoors, in a tennis stadium on courts made of clay and sand. In the middle of the tournament, the International Basketball Federation passed a rule that banned all players who were taller than 6'3"! The United States, who would have lost three players, objected and the rule was withdrawn. On the day of the final game, it rained and the courts turned into mud! Needless to say, the players found it difficult to dribble, and the score at the end of the game between the United States and Canada was a low 19–8. (The U.S. won.)

• In 1948, the Games were held in London, England. The basketball competition had some pretty bizarre highlights: A British referee was knocked unconscious during a preliminary game between Chile and Iraq. . . . A Chinese player scored a basket by dribbling between the legs of the seven-foot United States center, Bob Kurland. . . . In a match between Brazil and Mexico for third place, Alfredo Rodrigues da Motta of Brazil lost his pants and had to spend the rest of the match in the dressing room. . . . Iraq lost one game by 100 points!

• The 1960, United States basketball team was the greatest Olympic team ever assembled. Ten members of that team went on to play in the NBA! The original roster was: Jay Arnette, Walt Bellamy, Bob Boozer, Terry Dischinger, Jerry Lucas, Oscar Robertson, Adrian Smith, Burdette Haldorson, Darrall Imhoff, Allen Kelley, Lester Lane, and Jerry West. They won every game by at least 24 points!

• On Sunday, September 10, 1972, one of the greatest controversies in the history of sports took place at the Olympics in Munich, Germany. In a close match between the United States and the Soviet basketball teams, Soviet star Sasha Belov accidentally threw the ball to the United States's Doug Collins. With three seconds left in the game, Collins was fouled intentionally by a Soviet player. Collins went to the foul line and calmly sank two free throws, giving the United States its first lead of the game, 50–49. The Soviet team inbounded the ball but, two seconds later, the head referee noticed a disturbance at the scorer's table and called a time out. The Soviet coach claimed that he had called a time out after Collins's first free throw. One second remained, but the secretary-general of the Federal International Basketball Association — R. William Jones — intervened and ordered the clock set back three seconds. What Jones did was illegal. He had no right to make a ruling during a game — only a referee can do that. But Jones ruled the FIBA with an iron hand, and no one dared question him. Now, with four seconds left, the Soviet coach brought in Ivan Yedeshko who threw a long pass to Sasha Belov. Belov caught the pass perfectly and scored the winning basket.

• Losing that game against the Soviets under such false pretenses was bad enough, but for United States coach Hank Iba, things only got worse. Later, while he was arguing with officials and signing the official protest, Iba's wallet — containing $370 — was picked from his pocket!

MEDAL WATCH! Dream Team Scorecard

Fill in the winning countries each day and watch these sharpshooting nations race for the gold!

Quarterfinals	**Semifinals**	**Finals**
August 4, 1992	August 6, 1992	August 8, 1992

1st Place_____   1st Place_____   1st Place_____

2nd Place_____   2nd Place_____   2nd Place_____

3rd Place_____   3rd Place_____

4th Place_____   4th Place_____

5th Place_____

6th Place_____

7th Place_____

8th Place_____

THE WINNERS!

Gold Medal:_____   Silver Medal:_____   Bronze Medal:_____

Send a message! Write to your favorite player. Give
him your suport. Tell him to GO FOR THE GOLD!

(your favorite player)
USA Basketball
1750 East Boulder Street
Colorado Springs, CO 80909